THE NEW LADUVANE SONGBOOK

Original edition:
Design and transcriptions by Jane Peppler; editing by Anabel Graetz, Jana Buchholz, and Jane Peppler copyright 1977.

New edition:
Design, additional material by Jane Peppler copyright 2009.

Available from Skylark Productions:
http://skylark2.com 919-383-8952
or jane@mappamundi.com

Dedication 1977:

For our dear friend and teacher, Sveta Jones, in appreciation of her help and support.

Dedication 2009:

For Anabel Graetz, who changed the course of my life, and for all my other beloved singing companions in Mappamundi, Laduvane (especially Beth Holmgren), and the Yale Slavic Chorus.

Copyright 2009 by Jane Peppler

ISBN 978-0-9818115-2-9

All rights reserved. PLEASE contact me at jane@mappamundi.com for permission to copy any part of this publication. For purchase, see page 48.

Printed in the United States of America

1977 Forward

These are some of our favorite songs. They are all easy to learn, and they represent a wide variety of styles. Many of them are presented the way we sing them, in our own arrangements; others are presented as we found them, in the sources listed. Many are as villagers sing them; others are in more formal arrangements.

We have tried to be as accurate as possible with words and melodies, but we are involved in the folk process as singers, not scholars. Our music is living music; this is our invitation to you to join the process. How to start? First, yell "HEY!" as loud as you can - make sure the sound comes from your stomach, not your head or throat - then sing, loudly and clearly. Get some recordings of native singers - check the sources at the back of the book, for instance - listen, and note their pronunciation, *relax*, then sing and sing! - Anabel Graetz

2009 Forward

I was an alum of the Yale Slavic Chorus, a new college graduate uncertain of what might come next, when I first met Anabel Graetz in 1975. Hearing the sound of Laduvane waft over the greensward in Falmouth, Massachusetts, I decided to follow the sound to Cambridge and join the group. For many years I transcribed and arranged for Laduvane and specialized in singing drone (one note, more or less, throughout a whole song). We made two LPs with Stephen Michelson for Physical Records, and we made this songbook.

Over the years I have seen an astonishing number of bootlegs of this collection; when someone contacted me recently and actually offered to PURCHASE it, I was flabbergasted enough to find my one last remaining copy and typset it anew. Here it is, with the addition of some songs I've learned in the last 30+ years. - Jane Peppler

PLEASE do not xerox this book or its pages. It is available for purchase, easily, cheaply, from http://skylark2.com (see back page). Thank you.

INDEX:

Ajde Jano 6
Što e Ludo 8
Sadi Moma 10
Ličko Kolo 11
Prsten Mi Padna 12
Savo Vodo 14
Divojka Je 15
Zaspo Janko 16
Tri Jeterve 17
Vrličko Kolo 18
Mi Go Zatvorile 20
Dve Nevesti. 22
Banijsko Kolo 24
Danama. 26
Molih Ta 28
Otdavali Molodu. 29
Dobro Došle 30
Oj Poved Kolo 31
Daj Mi, Daj 32
Ej, Pletenice 33
Polegala. 34
Što Mi E Milo 36
Notes and Sources. 38
References 39
Pronunciation Guide 40
Na Pirino Mome 41
Na Ugorje. 42
Czerwone (instrumental) 43
Bisero Čerko 44
Oi Da Ty Kalinushka 46
Skylark Productions: Ordering Information 48

"The New Laduvane Songbook" available from Skylark Productions, http://skylark2.com

AJDE JANO

SERBIA

Ajde Jano, konje da prodamo
Ajde Jano, ajde dušo
Konje da prodamo

Ajde Jano, kuću da prodamo
Ajde Jano, ajde dušo
Kuću da prodamo

Da prodamo, samo da igramo
Da prodamo, Jano dušo
Samo da igramo

Come, Jana, dance the kolo!
Sell the horse, sell the house - only dance.

Shto e ludo

This is the only traditional canon we know of from the Balkans. It is sung and danced during the summer festivals.

Sto e ludo son sonilo
Na raka mu moma do, Na raka mu moma dojde

Pa mu voda podavaše
Koga se razbudi, Koga se razbudilo

Nima moma nima vraga
Zema ludo ruško no, Zema ludo ruško nošče

Da se bode da se gode
Pernitsa mu odgova, Pernitsa mu odgovara

"A bre ludo, ludo mlado,
Ne se body, ne se go, Ne se body ne se godi

"Ako ti e rečenitsa
Sama doma če ti do, Sama doma če ti dojde

"Če ti mete niz dvorove
Kako letna jarebi, Kako letna jarebitsa

"Kako letna jarebitsa
Kako zimna guguvi, Kako zimna guguvitsa."

A young man dreams that a young girl comes to him with water. When he wakes, the girl is gone. He takes a knife to stab himself, but his pillow says: "Young man, don't stab yourself. If you're lucky, she'll come alone to your house and sweep your yard like a dove."

Sadi Moma

Denja sadi dva se kaje (vinena libe...)

Prasnala bela loza (vinene libe...)

Nap'lnila devet buchvi s's vino lele s's vino

*A young girl planted a white grapevine.
When it matured, it filled nine barrels with wine.*

"Kaje" = ka-yeh; "s's" has a non-vowel, like a schwah.

Lichko Kolo

Lika - Dalmatia

K'o shto si sinoch, pyevao
Pod joye drage pendzherom
Moya ye draga zaspala
Studen yoy kamen pod glavom
Ya sam yoy kamen izmak'o
A svoyu ruku podmak'o

Sing to me, oh falcon, beneath my love's window.
She fell asleep; cold was the stone beneath her head.
I took away the stone, and there I placed my hand.

"The New Laduvane Songbook" available from Skylark Productions, http://skylark2.com

Prsten Mi Padna

Macedonia

This song is traditonally sung as a duet (the top two lines.) We added the drones and vary the combinations of lines - the song is always changing.

Otade reka male, otade reka
Otade reka male, vo pesochina

Vo pesochina male, vo pesochina
Vo pesochina male, na mesechina

Ovchar pomina male, ovchar pomina
Ovchar pomina male, toy mi go nayde

Taksay mu taksay nesho, sto kye mu taksash
Taksay mu taksay nesho, beloto litse

I da mu taksam male, I da mu taksam
I da mu taksam male, fayda si nema

I lost my ring by the side of the river, in the moonlight. A shepherd found it. "Give me something for it - give me your fair face!" "Nothing I give you would be enough."

SAVO VODO

CROATIA

Sa-vo vo-do hey, La-ne, sa-vo vo-do moy dra-ga-ne
Sa-vo vo-do poz-dra-vi mi dra - gog

Nek ne kosi, hej Lane, nek ne kosi, moj dragane
Nek ne kosi trave pokraj Save

Pokosit tse, hej Lane, pokosit tse, moj dragane
Pokosit ts moje kose plave

Da ne pije, hey Lane, da ne pije, moj dragane,
Da ne pije voda iz te, Save

Popit tse mi, hej Lane, popit tse mi, moj dragane,
Popit tse mi moje ochi plave

Waters of the Sava, greet my love. Don't let him cut the grass at the edge of the river, he will be cutting my fair hair. Don't let him drink your waters, Sava, he will be drinking my blue eyes.

Divojka Je

*A girl picked flowers, then fell asleep
Then she dreamed about her sweetheart
She gave him flowers to smell*

"The New Laduvane Songbook" available from Skylark Productions, http://skylark2.com

Zaspo Yanko

Garesnica - Croatia

Pod yablanom zlatnom granom
Svoje mile drage
Lepe moye crne ochi
Pogledayte na me

Ya otrgnem zlatnu granu …

Janko sleeps beneath the poplar. "Oh, my dear one, look at me."
I broke off a golden branch.

Tri Jeterve

Very free

STARI MIKANOUCI, CROATIA

Tri ye-ter-ve zhi-to zhe-le La-do le mi-le oy La-de oy!

Yedna zhela snop nazhela. Lado le...
Druga zhela dva nazhela, Lado le...
Trecha zhela tri nazhela, Lado le...
Pak su legle te hladuyu
Dok sa zhita rosa spade
Legle malo pa zaspale
U tome yih suntse zayde
Otud ide svekrushina
Na trulyavih koleshina
Kako ide, kleti stade
Sta ste legle, moje snashe
Sta ste legle, ne digle se

Three sisters-in-law, reaping wheat, decide to nap in the shade.
Their mother-in-law passes them and says:
"Lie there, my daughters-in-law, and never wake up!"

> This is one of many Balkan songs which invoke the name of Lado, the Sun God worshiped in the centuries before Christianity took hold.

Vrlicko Kolo

Lika - Dalmatia

This is the sung introduction to a silent kolo from an island off the Dalmation coast. The dance itself is performed to the rhythm of the dancers' feet.

Bilo veče bilo usred podne
Mi smo seke skupa vojovale
A za jednim obe tugovale
Dalmatintsi hrabri ste vojnici
Hrabro ste se borili u Litsi

We said we would sing here,
be it night or mid-day.
We are sisters, come as one to mourn.
Dalmations, you were brave soldiers;
bravely you fought in Lika.

Mi Go Zatvorile

MACEDONIA

The melody is the second line from the top. The higher A drone should rarely be sung, and only by one person. The second, 4th, and 8th bars are sung with a turn.

Vo zandani ima, voda do kolena
Voda do kolena, kosa do ramena

Koga dojde vreme, Jordan da se pušta
Pravo on si trga, vo negovo selo.

Koga dojde Jordan do domašni porti,
Dva pati mi čukna, tri pati mi vikna.

Koga go dočula, negovata majka
Porti otvorila, sina pregrnila.

Kade mi je majko, mojto verno libe,
Porti da otvori, mene da pregrne?

Tvojto verno libe snošti se omaži
Za tvojot komšija; za tvojot pobratim.

Jordan has been in prison until the water in the cell is up to his knees and his hair is down to his shoulders. Finally freed, he rushes home and is embraced by his mother, who explains why his true live is not there to open the door: she just married his best friend.

Dve Nevesti

Bulgaria

Melody over drone, a diaphonic ("two voices") mode, is an ancient Balkan style. Dissonant intervals are frequent; in fact, in Greece the word "diaphony" denotes "discord." This song is antiphonal as well, with two duos answering each other (hold your notes and let them overlap the entrance of the next pair).

Em go vodat em go kuršat
Po meždu e malka moma
Pa gi tiom popituva
Arno li e venčiloto
A nevesti otgovarjat:
"Oženi se - ta da vidiš!"

Two young brides are leading the kolo, swaying gracefully. A young girl between them asks what it's like to be married. Their answer: "Get married yourself - then you'll see!"

Banijsko Kolo

Pokuplje, Croatia

This song accompanies a drmes, a dance led by the village's lead singer, who would make up verses as she went along—some patriotic, some with pointed references to people and events of the village. Many verses get made up, often with no relation to each other. This is a good song to do with kids. We often add drones and extra parts for fun. Sing "op-shy" with a long i sound.

Zeleni se jorgovan
Moj je dragi partizan.

Sone strane morave
Čita cure novine

Jedna baba gurbava
Rado vi se udala

Oh my country! We are Slovenians. Green are the fields; my sweetheart is a partisan. One humpbacked grandmother would happily get married.

Danama

Rhythmic - speeds up to end
Georgia

This children's song is based on a pun: "danama" means both "rain" and "knife."

Jejilma muxli iqara,
peri itsvala qanama. Qanama, etc.

Chkhara purebits shemova
ikharos glekhis dzalama. Dzalama, etc.

Bneli gaapos natelma
boroti guli danama. Danama, etc.

Vints chwenze avi sitskvaskvas
guli gaupos danama. Danama, etc.

I lost our original translation! (Oops) but I found this online:

A sprinkling rain has fallen down and gently covered all the ground. As the morning light rips the night, so evil hearts are torn by knives. If you about us tell white lies, we'll rip your hearts out with our knives.

Molih Ta

Bulgaria

Ne mozhih, da ta izmolya, Da ma ni glavish ni zhenish
Da ma ni glavish ni zhenish, Barem lyoi saya godina
Barem lyoi saya godina, Lyoi sova leto proleto
Lyoi sova leto proleto, Dorde ni doide podzime.
Dorde ni doide podzime, Da sa zazbirat momine
Da sa zazbirat momine, Momine na puprelkine.
Leftera da si pohodya, Gizdilo da si ponosya.
A ti ma maicho yoglavi, Yoglavi, yoshte yozheni.

I asked you, mother, I begged you, but I couldn't persuade you, neither to promise me to someone, nor to marry me off, but to promise me one more year, so that I might gather with the other girls at the working parties, and walk proudly with them, showing off our fine embroidered dresses. But you, mother, promised me to someone, and married me off.

Otdavali Molodu

Fyodorov Sisters

Na chuzhuyu storonu vo chuzhu derevnyu
Vo chuzhu derevnyu vo bol'shuyu sem'yu
Kak v izbu to vedut prigovarivayut
Kak i svyokor govorit 'Nerabotnitsu vedut'
Kak svekrovka govorit 'Neugodnitsu vedut'
Kak i tyotki govoryat 'Neprovednitsu vedut'

In the house of your mother-in-law you can't do anything right.

Dobro Doshle

MACEDONIA - FIRFOV

Ey, sto doydovte, oy
Sto eden oydovte, sto doydovte
Sto eden oydovte, oy

Welcome brightly colored weddings guests.
You come one hundred - you leave one hundred and one.

> For a Macedonian wife, marriage meant exile from her own home and virtual slavery in her husband's. Note: the high note is actually supposed to be sort of supersonic.

Oj Poved Kolo

CROATIA

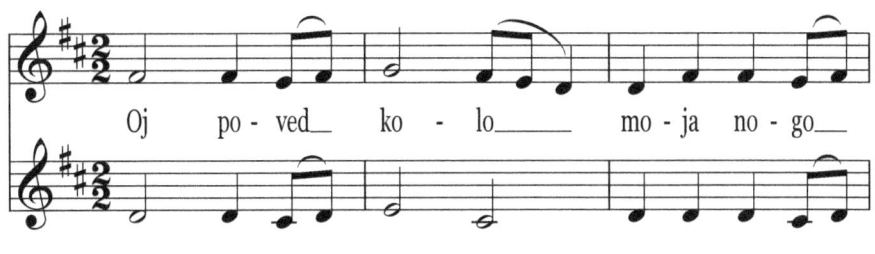

Oj stara lolo, jesi l'gdjegod zhiva
Oj bilo litse, i zhuta marama
Oj to pasira, nama Gundinkama
Oj kad poigra, mlada Shokadija
Oj pod njima se zemlitsa uvija

When the young Shokadians dance, the earth shakes beneath them!

From Gundinci, collected by Ethel Raim. Each verse is sung as a solo, and then repeated in harmony by all.
"Oj" = Oy; "moja" = mo-yah; "jesi" = yesi; "uvija" = uviya; "L'gdjegod" = lug-dyeh-god

Daj mi Daj

DALMATIA (PREVIC)

Daj mi, daj, daj mi, daj, o li-pa Ma-ri-ja. Daj mi, daj, daj mi, daj, za te-be lju-bim ja. Pri-di sme-noj pr-di sme-noj na mor-je, ve-slaj, ve-slaj Pri-di sme-noj kras-na je noch o-va

Bjonda si, bjonda si, ti lipa Marijo
Tebi tsu, tebi tsu, da pivam pismitsu

Give me your love, lovely Maria, and gladden beautifully this night.

> A love song, probably 19th or 20th century.
> As an experiment, I left the "j" in this song. "Daj" is pronounced "die" and "Marija" is Maria and "ljubim ja" is "lyubim ya" - "smenoj" is "smenoy," "morje" is "mor-yeh," "veslaj" uses long i (ves-lie like "lie down")

Ej, Pletenice

Ey zhi-to zhe-la Ba-ran-ka di-voi-ka
ey zhi-to-zhe-la Ba-ran-ka di-voy-ka
zviz-di-tse da-ni-tse Ne iz-la-zi
ra-no ye ra-no ye ra-no
ye zla-to mo-ye

Ej, pletenitse od uva do uva
zvizditse danitse, ne izlazi
rano je, rano je zlato moje

Ej, alaj mene, moja dika chuva

Ej, pletenitse, divojachko litse

Ej, a kapitse dobro vata lits

A girl from Baranja cut wheat. Hey, thick braids from ear to ear.
Little morning star, don't come out.
It's too early, too early my golden one My love looks after me.
Hey, braids and a girl's face A little cap frames the face well.

POLEGALA

CROATIA

Po - le - ga - la tra - va de - te - la Chur - lye - na ki - ti - tsa Ru - me - na ro - zi - tsa le - pa mo - ya li - va do ze - len

This folk song, like many others, is sung very freely. It was created by people unacquainted with the concept of a cumpulsory time signature. Don't worry about the beat; sing the song over and over until it flows unhurriedly.

Jo mi žela gizdava djevoj
Črljena kititsa, rumena rožitsa
Lepa moja livado zelen

Kaj nažela to pred kon' kedel
Črljena kititsa, rumena rožitsa
Lepa moja livado zelen

A harvest song from Croatia:
The grass has grown high
in my beautiful green field.
The proud girl will cut it
and feed it to the horse.

Sto mi e milo

Macedonia

Na k'epentsite, mamo, da sedam,
Stružkite momi, mamo, momi da gledam.
Lele varaj... etc
Stružkite momi, mamo, momi da gledam.

Koga na voda, voda mi odat,
So tija stomni, mamo, stomni šareni.
Lele varaj... etc.
So tija stomni, mamo, stomni šareni.

Na ovaj izvor, izvor studeni,
Tam da se združki, mamo, združki soberat.
Lele varaj... etc.
Tam da se združki, mamo, združki soberat.

How nice it would be to have a shop in Struga, to sit and watch the girls carry water in their colorful jars - to the well where the students meet.

Notes and Sources

We have indicated country, and where possible, village origin at the upper right of each song. If we've erred in omitting a credit, please let us know and we'll make the correction.

Many people have made this book possible: Jana Buchholz, who went to Otešovo and learned some of our favorite songs; Ron Gursky, who provided the words and music for Danama; people who have transcribed and arranged for Laduvane, including Lucy Sperber, Cindy Fogg, Joan Goodman, Janet Nelson, and Martin Graetz; other people who have given us songs, lyrics, inspirations: Vicky Campbell, Mary Wolfe, Ellen Rice, Martha Schechter, Dik Crum, Chuck Baber, Harry Brauser, Yves Moreau, Pece Atanasovski and Emil Cossetto.

Finally, an enormous thank you to Ethel Raim, who not only collected and introduced many of the songs in this book, but who has been invaluable in bringing this music to America and to us. Without her this book wouldn't be here.

References

Zivko Firfov - learned by Jana Buchholz at Otešovo, Macedonia, 1973

Lado - Opšaj Diri from "Lado: The Folk Dance and Folk Song Ensemble of Zagreb, Jugoslavia," Jugoton. Polegala from "Lado: The croatian Song & Dance Ensemble, Vol. 2, Monitor MFS 470.

Yves Moreau, recorded in Bulgaria on Worldtone Records

Ratimir Prević, Narodne Pjesme Jugoslavije za Harmoniku i Pjevanje, Vol. II, Zagreb 1963.

Ethel Raim: Dve Nevesti from The Pennywhistlers "A Cool Day and Cracked Corn;" Molih Ta from "Village Music of Bulgaria - A Harvest, A Shepherd, A Bride;" Što Mi E Milo from "The Pennywhistlers, Folksongs of Eastern Europe."

Joža Vlahović: Vrličko from Yugoslavia, Ivan Ivančan; Ajde Jano from "Pjesme Naroda Jugoslavia," Emil Cossetto

Dr. Vinko Žganec: Nada Sremec, Hrvatske Narodne Pjesme i Plesovi, Seljačka Sloga, Zagreb, 1951

PRONUNCIATION

The original book transliterated the lyrics into the Serbo-Croatian alphabet.

In 2009 I have kept to this practice except for most of the written sheet music itself, where I attempted by and large to go for a more foolproof phonetic spelling (after hearing too many people with our book happily singing "dawdzh" instead of "die" for the word "daj," for instance). The inconsistency is no doubt annoying but well-intentioned.

From the 1977 edition:

A as in b**A**ll
AJ, long i as in p**ie**
Ć and Č, as in pi**TCH**
DŽ as in ju**DGE**
E as in t**E**n
EJ long a as in h**EY**
G as in **G**oat
H as in Ba**CH**
I long e as in rav**I**ne

J, y as in **Y**olk
LJ, li as in bi**LI**ous
NJ ñ as in pi**NI**on
O as in h**O**rn
OJ oy as in t**OY**
R - flap, short trill
Š sh as in **SH**ip
U oo as in tr**UE**
Ž zh as in a**Z**ure

In Georgian (Danama is our only example), an apostrophe indicates a stopped consonant. X is the German "ch" and Q is a sounded version of "x."

Na Pirino Mome

Bulgaria

Ya sam si milo libe hubava, ya sam si milo libe gisdava
Oti sam rasla libe v'planina, oti sam rasla libe v'Pirina

Pirinska voda, libe, sam pila. Pirinska treva, libe, gazila.
Bulgarska mayka me e razhdala. Mayka Pirinka libe gledala.

Where am I walking on Pirin, why are you so beautiful, girl?
What mother has born you? What water have you drunk?
I am pretty dear love, I am beautiful dear love,
Because I have grown up in the mountains, grown up in Pirin.
I've drunk Pirin water, I've walked on Pirin grass
A Bulgarian mother has born me, Mother Pirin has raised me.

Na Ugorje Na Vjetru

Russia

Na u - gor - je na vje - tru.
Vje - tjer du - jet v'do - li - nu da raz - du -
va - jet v'rja - vi - nu,
rja - vi - nu zje - ljo - nu - ju

Na ravinje oden' prut
Na prutochkje kistochka da a na kistochkje jagodka
O naspjela zrjela

Na tupoj runa totchas
Mat' divchon'ku gladila da rusu kosu zapljela
Docher' zamuzhu dala

Docher' zamuzhu dala
Na chuzhuju storonu da a na chuzhuju storonu
Za Ivana sokola

Uzh ty sokol Vanjushka
Razudala golova da beregi khozhu nozhku
Na chuzhoj storonushkje

Wind blows into the valley and grove. In the grove there is a branch and on the branch a berry, o so ripe. The mother strokes the girl and braids her hair. She is giving her daughter in marriage, into another country, to Ivan the eagle. Oh you are an eagle, Vanyushka. She unleashed her head and went on another shore, to a foreign land.

Czerwone

Polish

Bisero Cerko

MACEDONIA

Turchin ot vera mori ne znaye lele
Turchin vo crkva mori ne ide
Bisero lele
Turchin vo crkva mori ne ide

Ako ye ot Boga recheno lele
Turska nevesta mori che stanam
Maychitse mori
Turska nevesta lele che stanam

Turska nevesta dzhanam che stanam lele
So devet rala mori tapani
Maychitse mori
So tija piskavi zurli

Pearl, dear daughter, don't embrace the Turk. A Turk knowns nothing of our faith -- a Turk doesn't go to church. "If God wills it, I'll become a Turkish bride, dear mother, with nine pairs of drums, with those strident zurlas."

Oi Da Ty Kalinushka

A. Novikova

Oi da ty ka - li - nu - shka ty ma-
Oi da nje spu - shchai li - sta__ vo si -
Oi da ka - ra - bjel'__ ply - vjot__ azh vo -

-li - nu - shka, Oi da ty nje stoi____ nje
-nje__ ma - rje Oi da vo si - njem - to ma-
-da__ rje - vjot Oi da kak na tom__ ka - ra -

stoi na go - rje_____ kru - toi.
rje ka - ra - bjel'_____ ply - vjot
blje dva pol - ka_____ sol - dat

Available from Skylark Productions

Skylark Productions offers songbooks and cds of traditional and early music. For details and ordering information visit our website. Here's a sample from:

http://skylark2.com

Songbooks:

Let Memory Keep Us All - The Solstice Assembly Songbook. *"Really old songs"* in choral arrangements for mixed voices.

The Triangle Jewish Chorale Songbook - *Thirty-nine Jewish songs in Hebrew, Yiddish, Ladino, and English in choral arrangements for mixed voices.*

Songs for Non-Singers Songbook Series - *see the website for details.*

Compact Discs:

We Did It, Rag Faire, Early Fare, Hearts' Delight - The Pratie Heads - "More or Less Traditional" *music from the British Isles.*

World Music Our Way - Mappamundi. *Eastern European, Yiddish, English, and more!*

Three Log Night, Under the Drawbridge, Some Assembly Required - The Solstice Assembly - *a wide variety of choral music, a cappella and with the Band of Ages*

Sedgefield Fair - Jane Peppler, Jacqueline Schwab, Robbie Link - *tradional songs from England and Scotland.*

www.ingramcontent.com/pod-product-compliance
Lightning Source LLC
Chambersburg PA
CBHW031436040426
42444CB00006B/846